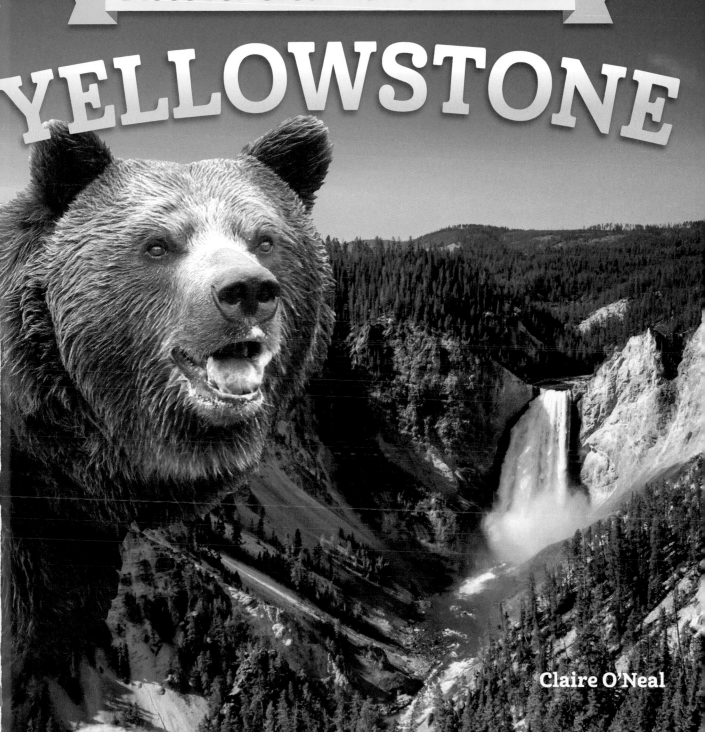

Discover Great National Parks:
YELLOWSTONE

Claire O'Neal

Kids' Guide to History, Wildlife, Geysers, Hiking, and Preservation

© 2024 by Curious Fox Books™, an imprint of Fox Chapel Publishing Company, Inc., 903 Square Street, Mount Joy, PA 17552.

Discover Great National Parks: Yellowstone is a revision of *Yellowstone*, published in 2017 by Purple Toad Publishing, Inc. Reproduction of its contents is strictly prohibited without written permission from the rights holder.

Paperback ISBN 979-8-89094-070-4
Hardcover ISBN 979-8-89094-071-1

The Cataloging-in-Publication Data in on file with the Library of Congress.

To learn more about the other great books from Fox Chapel Publishing, or to find a retailer near you, call toll-free 800-457-9112 or visit us at www.FoxChapelPublishing.com.

We are always looking for talented authors. To submit an idea, please send a brief inquiry to acquisitions@foxchapelpublishing.com.

Fox Chapel Publishing makes every effort to use environmentally friendly paper for printing.

Printed in China

WELCOME

CHAPTER ONE
AMERICA'S
BEST IDEA

In 1872, the U.S. Congress considered Yellowstone to be such a special place that they designated it as the world's first national park. Over 150 years later, the weird and wonderful nature of Yellowstone National Park still stands apart. In fact, visiting Yellowstone is like visiting three parks in one. It is a living museum of history, geology, and ecology. In Yellowstone, you can stay in one of the world's largest log cabins, the 119-year-old Old Faithful Inn. Out on the trail, imagine the harsh, wild terrain battled by America's legendary "mountain men." Marvel at the native-made wikiup tents that still stand along Wickiup Creek.

Yellowstone's amazing geology scared away some native settlers who believed the place to be cursed. The mysterious land smoked and fumed, and sometimes the whole earth seemed to quake with the rage of gods. What is the source of Yellowstone's mystery? It sits atop one of the world's largest volcanoes. The heat from the Yellowstone Volcano powers more thermally active geologic features than anywhere else in the world.

Old Faithful was given its name because of its regular eruptions around twenty times a day.

One, the famous Old Faithful Geyser, blasts superheated water nearly 180 feet into the sky around twenty times a day.

Yellowstone's rich wildlife always puts on a show worth watching. Its Lamar Valley has been called "America's Serengeti," after the African plains that are world-famous for safaris. Whether hearing a male elk bugle its mating call or spotting a grizzly bear snacking on wild berry bushes, Yellowstone offers a rare opportunity to see wild animals in their natural habitat.

Yellowstone truly offers something for everyone, largely because of the park's size. Its 2.2 million acres make it larger than the states of Rhode

Grizzly bears fiercely guard their young. Never approach a bear, especially when there are cubs nearby.

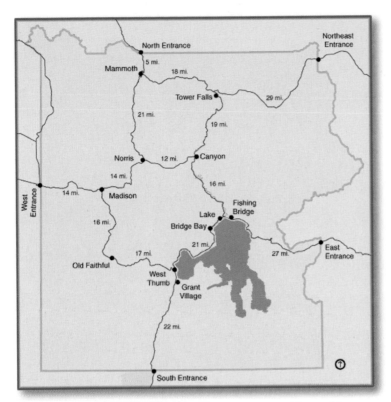

Yellowstone covers a large geographic area and has five entrances.

Island and Delaware combined. It covers the northwest corner of Wyoming and spills over into Montana and Idaho.

Scientists study how Yellowstone's animals migrate over the seasons. They point out that the park is part of a much larger region that deserves special attention. The Greater Yellowstone Ecosystem spans over eighteen million acres of unique climate and geography. Its plant and animal species make up one of the largest unbroken temperate ecosystems remaining on Earth. Yellowstone and the neighboring Grand Teton National Park—along with seven national forests, nearly a dozen national wilderness areas, and other state and local parks—work together to protect the Greater Yellowstone Ecosystem.

Called "America's Best Idea," the idea of a national park caught on quickly. As of 2023, the United States has sixty-three national parks spread across thirty states. Nations all over the world have created national parks, too, to preserve and protect their own national treasures. But Yellowstone National Park was the world's first celebration of

Protecting America's natural wonders has been a concern of many American presidents, including President Barack Obama, for well over one hundred years.

wilderness. Over five generations of Americans have made the trek—then by wagon or train, today by car or RV—to this remote corner of Wyoming to marvel at its wonders. After 150 years, Yellowstone remains the most popular U.S. national park. Over 3.9 million visitors explored its magic in 2022, and a record-breaking 4.8 million visitors came to Yellowstone in 2021.[1] Come along and find out why.

KIDS CAN: BE A JUNIOR RANGER!

Kids visiting Yellowstone, or any other U.S. National Park, can sign up for the Junior Ranger program at any visitor center. If you do, you'll get a workbook to guide the whole family through fun activities that also help you explore the park. Complete the workbook, go on a hike, and join in on an educational Park Ranger program. Soon you, too, will earn a Junior Ranger badge, one specially made and available only at that national park. Together with a park ranger, you'll take this pledge:

"As a junior park ranger, I promise to learn all I can to help preserve and protect Yellowstone's wildlife, history, and natural features. When I return home, I will teach others how to protect the natural world."

If you can't visit Yellowstone, you can still earn a Junior Ranger patch through the National Park service Junior Ranger Online program (www.nps.gov/kids/junior-ranger-online.htm). On the website, you can learn about U.S. National Parks and play online games to test your park smarts. Do well, and the Park Service will mail you a badge of your own!

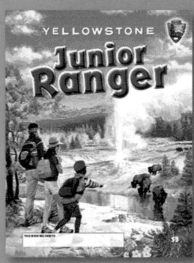

Junior Ranger guides can be picked up at one of the visitors centers.

CHAPTER TWO
THE WORLD'S FIRST
NATIONAL PARK

When the Lewis and Clark Expedition set out to explore the enormous, uncharted wilderness of the western United States, they asked John Colter to come along. From 1803 to 1806, Meriwether Lewis, William Clark, Colter, and other men traveled by foot and by boat from the Mississippi River all the way to the Pacific Ocean. An expert hunter and canoe builder, Colter saved the team from dangerous Indian encounters more than once.

On the way back, Colter heard the Rocky Mountains calling him to stay behind. Some thought he was crazy. Most thought he would die, whether from hostile Indians, fierce wild animals, or the harsh mountain winters. He not only lived, but during the winter of 1806–1807, he became the first white man to explore the Yellowstone region of the Rocky Mountains.

He returned to the East in 1810 with stories of strange and beautiful wonders. In this land that the Native American Crow tribe called *Mi tsi a-da-zi,* or Rock Yellow River, Colter saw natural fountains shooting plumes of

The Lower Yellowstone Falls are nearly twice as tall as Niagara Falls (308 feet high).

John Colter was amazed at the natural formations of Yellowstone.

boiling water hundreds of feet into the air. He saw painted puddles of hot mud bubbling and burping like witches' cauldrons. He watched waterfalls tumble down high cliffs of yellow rock, disappearing into rainbow mist.

After Colter wandered through, other white men followed. Fur trappers hunted animals like beaver, whose pelts were greatly valued as fabric for fancy hats back East. They could make a good living—if they survived. Sometimes the hunted animals, like bear and cougar, would hunt back. Hardy men like Jim Bridger and Osborne Russell became living legends, roaming the rocky wilderness alone as the original "mountain men." They braved subzero nighttime temperatures in every season but summer, and fed themselves using little more than a knife and a pot. Many learned to speak several Native American languages and became friendly with local tribes.

Gold prospectors followed the fur trappers. Many of these fortune-seekers returned broke in their pockets but rich in stories of a special place known as Yellow Stone, where the earth came alive.

Jim Bridger was a famous mountain man from the 1800s.

The Hayden survey pack train visited Mirror Lake in 1871 to conduct scientific research.

In 1871, the U. S. government sent a team of scientists to Yellowstone. Led by Ferdinand V. Hayden of the U.S. Geological Survey, they went to see for themselves if Yellowstone's sights were fact or fiction. The team returned with an unusual idea. What if, instead of tossing Yellowstone's land up for grabs to new American settlers, the U.S. government kept it and protected it? Congress agreed, and on March 1, 1872, President Ulysses S. Grant signed a law that set aside Yellowstone's land "for the benefit and enjoyment of the people." That's when Yellowstone became the world's first national park.

Since the idea of a national park was so new, the government left it up to the park's first manager, Nathaniel P. Langford, to imagine what Yellowstone should be. Langford was a natural choice. He helped lead an 1870 expedition to explore Yellowstone, where fellow explorer Henry Washburn gave the Old Faithful geyser its name.[1] Langford also

Nathaniel P. Langford was Yellowstone's first manager.

climbed to the top of what would be named Mount Langford, a 10,623-foot peak. But he could not run a park when the government refused to send him any money or employees. He soon left to seek his fortune elsewhere.

In 1877, the government put Philetus Norris, a fur trapper and pioneer, in charge. This time they paid $10,000 a year (about $227,000 in today's dollars). Norris hired Yellowstone's first park ranger who would preserve the park's grounds and protect its wildlife from poachers. Norris expanded Yellowstone's roads so that wagons could reach Geyser Basin and Mammoth Hot Springs. His work excited businessman Jay Cooke, the founder of the Northern Pacific Railroad. Cooke cooked up a grand scheme to build a hotel inside the park, with a railroad that would bring tourists straight to the geyser. Norris refused to allow the project for fear that Cooke's plans would damage the park.

Norris did not know that Cooke had secret, corrupt government friends. They had promised the Northern

At Mammoth Hot Springs, hot water has formed colorful cliffs over milenia.

Pacific some land inside the beautiful new park. In exchange, these dirty officials would receive part of the railroad's profits. Cooke's friends swiftly replaced the honest Norris with new park managers. They wrote illegal contracts that allowed Northern Pacific to chop down forests and give away land. They even used the meat from the park's elk and deer to feed railroad workers.[2] With no protection for the park, visitors used dynamite to fish in Yellowstone Lake. Some broke off chunks of rock to take home as souvenirs.[3]

Cooke's plan was exactly the opposite of what Yellowstone was meant to be. Luckily, businessman and environmental champion Stephen Mather stepped in. He told Washington, D.C. about the catastrophe at Yellowstone. Congress sent the U.S. Army to stop the corruption. Between 1886 and 1918, the soldiers transformed the park. They started with their headquarters, Fort Yellowstone. This outpost still stands at Mammoth Hot Springs.

U.S. Army engineer Lieutenant Daniel Kingman designed and built Yellowstone's Grand Loop, a figure-eight road that paved the way for cars to visit Yellowstone's greatest sights with the least environmental impact possible. The soldiers felt a strong sense of duty to protect the land. They worked hard to protect Yellowstone's wildlife from poachers, to prevent

Fort Yellowstone, Officer's Quarters.

Grand Loop gives drivers a panoramic view of the park.

tourists from damaging its geologic formations, and to keep any wildfires under control.

In 1916, Congress created the National Park Service. New park rangers took over the soldiers' job. They have kept the soldiers' strong sense of duty alive. Their mission is to preserve and protect parklands for everyone to enjoy.

U.S. President Gerald Ford—the only president to serve as a National Park Ranger—spent "one of the best summers of my life" in Yellowstone in 1936. The then-23-year-old worked at the Canyon Hotel and Lodge and as an armed guard at Yellowstone's bear-feeding truck.[4]

PREHISTORIC YELLOWSTONE

Though the land seemed vast and empty, John Colter was by no means the first to see Yellowstone. Blackfeet, Crow, Shoshone, Bannock, and other Native American tribes all occupied territory around Yellowstone. Their ancestors had lived in the area for at least 11,000 years. Prehistoric people carved black volcanic glass from Yellowstone's Obsidian Cliffs into arrowheads. At Mummy Cave near the eastern entrance of Yellowstone, archaeologists have found hides, stone hunting tools, and a 9,000-year-old mummy.

Possible Native American rock shelter.

Native hunters walked well-worn trails into Yellowstone to get to prime hunting and fishing grounds. They built pole tents, known as wikiups, of lodgepole pine trunks and branches. Some wikiups stayed as permanent shelters. They can still be seen along Wickiup Creek.

A group of Shoshone, the hardy Tukudika people, lived in Yellowstone for at least 1,000 years. The Tukudika were skilled hunters and fishermen. Yellowstone's bighorn sheep made a tasty meal for them. Its thick woolly coat and horns could be fashioned into bows and other tools. In the 1870s, the U.S. government rounded up the few that remained in Yellowstone. They were moved to the Wind River Indian Reservation in central Wyoming.[5]

CHAPTER THREE
A GEOLOGY
WONDERLAND

Nestled atop the Rocky Mountains, Yellowstone is nearly surrounded by sharp peaks. The sky-piercing Absaroka Range guards the entire eastern border of the park. Its highest mountain, Eagle Peak, crests at 11,358 feet. The Gallatin Range forms part of the western border of the park and stretches into Montana. Even Yellowstone's flat plains are far above sea level, with an average elevation of 8,000 feet. Yellowstone is so high that the Continental Divide runs across the park's southwest corner. Water west of the Divide flows to the Pacific Ocean. Water to its east makes its way to the Mississippi River and empties into the Gulf of Mexico.

Yellowstone's mountain ranges make for majestic scenery. But the magic of Yellowstone lies simmering under the mountains. When you visit the park, you stand atop one of the largest, most explosive volcanoes on the planet. Around fifty million years ago, eruptions buried Yellowstone's ancient redwood forests. Ash petrified the trees, which stand in the Tower-Roosevelt area of

Yellowstone Lake is America's largest mountain lake. It is a popular spot for boating.

Tree trunks from long ago turned into a type of fossil called petrified wood.

the park. The Yellowstone Supervolcano exploded again 2.1 million years ago. In one of the most powerful volcanic eruptions in earth's history, it shot ash and rock over 5,790 square miles.[1]

Magma has erupted several times throughout Yellowstone's history. An oval-shaped caldera remains from a violent eruption 600,000 years ago. It is twenty-eight by forty-seven miles across.[2] After another eruption 70,000 years ago, lava filled in a plain in the northern Rockies, creating Yellowstone's high plateau.

Park geologists believe that the volcano will erupt again, and with devastating force. When? No one can say. For now, geologists watch this volcano's quiet power, looking every day for signs of another eruption.

Yellowstone's ground may appear normal to visitors, but having magma so close to the surface can make the ground surprisingly hot. Heating and cooling pushes the ground up and down, cracking the Earth's crust. In some places, steam or volcanic gas bubbles up through these cracks into lakes or riverbeds, creating hot springs. The Grand

Brilliant colors are found at the Grand Prismatic Spring. They are caused by unusual types of bacteria that live in hot water.

Prismatic Spring, the world's third largest hot spring, delights the eye with its striking rainbow of color. The vivid colors come from unusual bacteria that thrive in the superheated temperatures. Occasionally, even permanent mud puddles get hot enough to boil. At Mud Volcano and Fountain and Artists' Paint Pots, mud and silt bubble, plop, and

Mud pots erupt boiling hot mud. Unusual volcanic features like this are found throughout Yellowstone National Park.

gurgle with superheated gases. In Boiling River and Firehole Canyon (which is only open in the summer), visitors can go swimming even during January snows.

In other places, rain and melting snow trickle down through the crust cracks. The trapped water then meets hot, molten rock; the water turns into steam and races to escape. Vents called fumaroles carry the steam, along with other hot volcanic gases and groundwater, to the surface. Yellowstone National Park boasts the world's largest collection of geysers—actually half the world's total—in one spot.[3]

GRAND TETON NATIONAL PARK

Many visitors to Yellowstone also stop at Grand Teton National Park, only about an hour's drive south. At every turn, mountains seem to burst out of the flat ground and soar to the sky. Jenny Lake reflects snow-capped Tetons in its mirror-flat water. Hikers can take a boat across the lake to access the trail to Inspiration Point for inspiring views of mountains and meadows. Visitors can travel by water in other ways, canoeing in Colter Bay or lazily floating down the Snake River on a tube raft.

Some prefer Grand Teton to Yellowstone, partly because Grand Teton is far less crowded than Yellowstone, even in the busiest month of July. With fewer touristy hot spots, Grand Teton invites visitors to slow down, relax, and enjoy spectacular views. They can also see deer, elk, antelope, bison, and sometimes bears.

Jenny Lake is a beautiful location near the Grand Tetons.

Chapter Four
A LIVING WILDLIFE
LABORATORY

Yellowstone's founders sought to protect the land for its show-stopping geology. In doing so, they also created a wildlife preserve. People from all over the world were settling in the United States, building cities that often pushed animals out of their habitats. Meanwhile, Yellowstone remained undisturbed. Yellowstone's long life gives wildlife biologists an important place to observe nature's long-term cycles.

Protected as it is, Yellowstone is not isolated. The property and needs of hunters and of farmers must be balanced against the need to preserve Yellowstone's wildlife. By listening to nature and to neighbors, park rangers try to make choices that preserve and protect this sensitive ecosystem.

Where the Buffalo Roam

Mountain meadows and the banks of the Yellowstone River provide ample food for Yellowstone's nearly 6,000 bison. These mighty wild animals are a symbol of the

Millions of bison used to roam the American west.

Bison might look cuddly, but they are wild animals. Keep your distance!

American West. Yellowstone visitors can watch the largest free-ranging buffalo herd in the world roam the plains. These mammals can grow to six feet tall and weigh up to one ton. Though massive, they seem tiny and playful as they roll around in dust or kick it up to keep cool and ward off insects. But there is no denying their size when herds of them plod across Yellowstone's popular roads, causing traffic jams on the Grand Loop.

By 1900, bison almost disappeared from the Lamar Valley. White settlers traveling west in the 1800s sought the thick, shaggy coats that help bison fend off predators and survive the harsh, cold winters. The settlers killed off bison from a population of millions to near extinction. In 1902, Yellowstone park ecologists hoped to bring the bison back to its former glory. They brought in twenty-one bison to add to a slow-growing population of only fifty. Today, over 420,000 bison live in the American West, thanks in large part to the protection of herds in national parks.

Lone Wolf

Wolves once roamed free in North America, living nearly everywhere north of central Mexico. Like medium-sized dogs, Yellowstone's gray, black, or white wolves can stand as high as three feet at the shoulders. They can measure up to six feet long from nose to tail. Packs of two to eleven wolves expertly hunt deer and elk, though they will also eat smaller mammals, such as beavers and voles.

Cattle ranchers who settled the western United States and Canada feared the gray wolf would kill their herds. Local governments encouraged people to hunt wolves. By 1960, gray wolves could be found only in the US in Alaska and Minnesota. The northern Rocky Mountain wolf was listed as an endangered species in 1973. In 1994, there were no wolves in Yellowstone. Worried wildlife biologists knew the important role of wolves. They are a keystone species of the Greater Yellowstone

Large animals, like bears and wolves, live in Yellowstone.

Wolves are now back
in Yellowstone.

Yellowstone Ecosystem. Wolves work together to bring down prey that other predators can't kill. Wolf-killed carcasses provide food for other species, from ravens to coyotes and even bears. Also, having gray wolves around actually helps deer and elk populations. When they hunt sick and weak animals, they leave behind healthier and stronger herds overall.

Yellowstone's park ecologists won over officials at the U.S. Department of the Interior, who agreed to a wolf repopulation plan. In the winters of 1995 and 1996, thirty-one new wolves were brought in from outside the park. The wolves flourished in the Lamar Valley. By 2011, the gray wolf was no longer considered endangered. In 2014, Yellowstone ecologists estimated that between 400 and 450 wolves were living in the park. Many consider the rebounded wolf population to be one of Yellowstone's greatest success stories.[1] Since 1995, the Yellowstone Wolf Project program conducts year-round research, works to preserve native species, and educates people worldwide on wolf conservation.

Wildfire!

The summer of 1988 was Yellowstone's driest on record. Lightning struck Storm Creek on June 14 and sparked some of the dry wood ablaze. Gusty winds tossed the flames about, and more lightning struck the trees. By June 30, four fires burned in the backcountry. The drought continued, and more fires began. By July 21, the smoke began to affect park visitors. People across the country complained about the National Park Service's "Let It Burn" policy. Even President Ronald Reagan wondered why fires were ever allowed to burn in our national parks.[2] Under mounting pressure, the Park Service called in firefighters to put out all fires. But it was too late.

By August, firefighters were barely able to keep larger fires under control. On August 20, "Black Saturday," thick smoke choked common

The wildfire in 1988 destroyed hundreds of thousands of acres in Yellowstone.

visiting areas. Wind gusts up to sixty miles per hour whipped the fire across more than 150,000 acres.[3] The flames licked at Old Faithful on September 7, threatening Yellowstone's historic buildings.

In the end, only nature could stop what it started. The first blanket of snow on September 11 finally brought the blaze under control.

More than 25,000 firefighters and military personnel worked tirelessly to keep the wildfire under control.

The fire spread to treetops and became crown fires.

They saved all the park's buildings, including the Old Faithful Inn.[4] In the end, the fire burned through 1.2 million acres of parkland. No visitors, staff, or firefighters lost their lives.

Surprisingly, the fire had little effect on large animal populations. Only nine bison, four mule deer, two moose, two grizzlies, and one black bear died. Nearly 250 elk were lost—out of a population of over 30,000—and around 100 of those had been struck by fire-fighting vehicles.

The media proclaimed the tragic loss of Yellowstone's forests. Many people thought careless visitors tossing matches or cigarettes or leaving campfires had started the fires. In fact, most of 1988's fires started naturally, with lightning strikes setting old, dead, dry trees ablaze.

Natural wildfires are an important part of forest renewal, something many in the public did not understand. For example, Yellowstone's

Despite the efforts of 25,000 firefighters, it was not until the rain and snows came in September 1988 that the fires were finally put out.

lodgepole pine has special adaptations for living through fires. Some of its pinecones are sealed with a special sap that melts only at very high temperatures. The intense heat of a fire helps the pinecone release its seeds. The fire burns the mother tree to ash, making rich soil where new seedlings can sprout.

Ecologists have now had over thirty-five years to observe the positive effects of the 1988 blaze. Wildlife diversity in the forest is higher than ever. Lodgepole pine seedlings grow once more. These young trees are home to mountain bluebirds, woodpeckers, and many other nesting bird species.[5] Where thick lodgepole forests once blocked out the sun, grasses and wildflowers now grow. The tender plants are an important food source for Yellowstone's elk, deer, bison, and bears. Now, with a firsthand understanding of wildfire in nature's endless renewal, park officials stand ready to let Yellowstone burn responsibly.

A bull elk explores a burned area.

BEAR AWARE

Grizzly bears roam the high mountain plains at dawn and dusk, prowling for food. They inspire awe and fear. An eight-foot-tall adult grizzly can weigh up to 700 pounds. It can sprint at up to thirty-five miles per hour.

Black bears also live in Yellowstone. They are smaller than grizzlies—about the same height as a grown human—but can still weigh up to 600 pounds. Most have inky black fur, but black bears can be blond or even brownish red.

Grizzly bears find food with their sense of smell.

Bears hibernate between November and March or April. They wake up on a mission to eat as much as possible—they only get a few months to pack on weight before winter. All bears are omnivores. They love acorns and berries, but also eat meat like fish and elk.

Bear-aware visitors know that most bear encounters in Yellowstone end peacefully. Park rangers ask hikers to strap on "bear bells" that make noise as they walk to scare bears away. They also advise people to hike in groups. Since 1970, only nine percent of bear attacks happened to groups of three or more hikers.[6]

Chapter Five
ADVENTURE ALL
YEAR LONG

Yellowstone brings spectacular scenery, active wildlife, and a nonstop show of Earth's geology all year round. When is the best time for your family to visit Yellowstone? Any time! Yellowstone stays open all year, but while you can go into the park in the winter, much of it is closed. Each season brings changes and experiences that make the park seem brand new. To guarantee your family has the best experience, come prepared for anything. After all, you are entering America's oldest wilderness.

Most people visit during Yellowstone's short summer, from mid-July to mid-August. Every year, millions of visitors pass through Yellowstone's gates.[1] They drive nearly 290,000 cars—more than 9,000 cars per day. With that many people choking the Grand Loop, Yellowstone sometimes seems less like a wilderness and more like a rush-hour traffic jam. Never fear: visitors can get their dose of wildlife without leaving their car, since herds of bison crossing the street are often what causes the traffic! Remember, too, that Yellowstone has size on its side. A simple hike is often enough to leave the crowds behind.

Snow can pile up deep in Yellowstone in the winter months. It sometimes stays until June.

Watch out for bison taking over the road!

People brave the crowds of summer for a reason. High elevations keep the temperatures comfortable. At its warmest in July, Yellowstone barely breaks 80°F. Nights are cool, perfect for sleeping-bag snuggling in a tent. In any other season, the threat of snow at night can make tent camping dangerous for the unprepared.

Be ready for quick-changing weather at any time of year. Daytime thunderstorms can roll over the mountains quickly, soaking everything in a flash. At night in higher, mountainous spots, temperatures can plunge below freezing.

As autumn falls, so does the number of visitors. Temperatures are a bit lower, with an average high of 51°F in October. In September, the average low dips below freezing. The park also sees fewer hours of daylight. However, many easy delights remain. For example, fall is elk mating season, bringing with it loud bugle calls and interesting behavior from males. As long as the snow holds off, fall hiking is unbeatable, when turning leaves seem to paint the mountains with picture-perfect color.

A hike along the South Rim Trail has something for everyone. As the path traces the steep ledges of the Grand Canyon of the Yellowstone, hikers can feast their eyes on forest views, hot springs and mud pots, and also sweeping scenes of the canyon, including an overlook of Lower and the Upper Falls. Looking for more of a workout? Uncle Tom's Trail is not for the faint of heart—literally. Hikers fit enough to climb up and down a steep flight of 328 stairs are rewarded with a view so close to the Lower Falls they can feel the mist on their skin.

Summer and fall are great times to go hiking in Yellowstone.

Winter comes quick and blustery to the mountains. The average *high* in January is 24°F. Snow-seekers should come prepared for extremes, like Yellowstone's record-breaking low of −66°F. Snows can dust the meadow as early as mid-September. With an average of 150 inches of snowfall per year, it can take until mid-June to melt.[2] All entrances stay open to snowmobiles or snow coaches (buses with tracked tires)—but only the North Entrance stays plowed year-round to allow cars.

Yellowstone's winter visitors can also strap on their snowshoes or cross-country skis to get around. If you don't mind the chill, winter in Yellowstone presents a spectacular landscape of icy wonder. Ice three feet thick coats Yellowstone Lake between early December and late May. The volcano stays active deep inside the earth, so hot springs bubble

Yellowstone Lake freezes in winter and thaws again every summer.

on merrily, melting the snow. Geysers continue their fountain displays, creating icy artwork where the water lands. And the thermometer drops low enough to turn Lower and Upper Falls into a storybook collection of giant icicles.

Whenever you visit, Yellowstone offers a chance to escape from hectic modern life. Cell phone signals are spotty at best. Visitors simply must put down their phones, laptops, and daily stress and connect with their wild side. All who come prepared to enter Yellowstone and embrace the quiet gifts of nature leave rewarded with the experience of a lifetime.

TO PRESERVE . . . OR POLLUTE?

The rainbow colors of Morning Glory Pool—in gold, orange, and green—delight Yellowstone visitors today. Many don't realize that the hot spring was once a brilliant blue. In the past, excited vacationers threw coins into the pool for luck. Others threw in rocks and sometimes trash. Over time, pollution choked the mouth of the hot spring. Its temperature dropped and rainbow-colored bacteria began to grow, creating the hues of the spring today.

Even with extensive signs and education, pollution remains a problem. In August 2014, a tourist crashed his camera-equipped drone into Grand Prismatic Spring—despite a nationwide ban on remote-controlled aircraft in America's national parks.[3] Besides leaving a mess when they crash, drones cause noise pollution. They can interrupt the wilderness experience that many visitors are looking for in the park.

Pollution happens in less obvious ways, too. Cars clogging the Grand Loop sometimes create enough air pollution to spoil the mountain views. Streetlamps and storefront lights that shine into the night may disappoint skywatchers who visit Yellowstone. The lights may also confuse birds and bats.

Morning Glory Pool with its vibrant yellow and green colors.

FUN FACTS

- Yellowstone was established as the first national park in the world on March 1, 1872.

- It consists of 2.2 million acres, making it the second largest park in the continental United States.

- Yellowstone National Park is located in northwest Wyoming, reaching into Idaho and Montana.

- There are five entrances: North Entrance, near Gardiner, Montana; West Entrance, near West Yellowstone, Montana; South Entrance, near Jackson, Wyoming; East Entrance, near Cody, Wyoming; Northeast Entrance, near Silver Gate and Cooke City, Montana.

- The North Entrance is the only entrance kept open to cars all year round. The other four entrances are not plowed in the winter, but are open to snowmobiles from around mid-December to mid-March.

- Most visitors come between mid-July and mid-August each year.

- Highest point: Eagle Peak at 11,372 feet (3,466 meters).

- Average temperatures range from 9°F in January to 80°F in July.

FUN FACTS

- Yellowstone Volcano is one of the largest active volcanoes in the world.

- Over 2,400 miles of rivers, creeks, and streams run through Yellowstone.

- Hikers can walk over 900 miles of trails.

- Yellowstone is best known for thermal geology and wildlife preservation.

- Yellowstone Lake is the largest high-altitude lake in North America, at 7,732 feet above sea level.

- Water at Lower Falls of the Yellowstone River drops 308 feet, making it one of the highest waterfalls in North America.

- At least 406 species of thermophile algae and bacteria have been identified in the park.

- Of the nearly 300 bird species that have been sighted in Yellowstone, about 150 nest there, including the rare whooping crane.

- There are sixty-seven mammal species, including the threatened Canada lynx and grizzly bear, and the endangered gray wolf.

Sources: Yellowstone National Park website, U.S. National Park Service, www.nps.gov/yell *Fodor's Yellowstone and Grand Teton National Parks.* Eds. Debbie Harmsen, Michael Nalepa. New York: Random House Inc., 2010.

Chapter 1. America's Best Idea

1. U.S. National Park Service, "Visitor Use Statistics," https://irma.nps.gov/Stats/Reports/Park

Chapter 2. The World's First National Park

1. Aubrey L. Haines, *Yellowstone National Park: Its Exploration and Establishment* (Washington, D.C.: U.S. Department of the Interior, 1974)

2. Don Pitcher, *Moon Handbooks: Yellowstone & Grand Teton* (Emeryville, CA: Avalon Travel Publishing, 2006), pp. 313–314.

3. Ibid., p. 314.

4. Yellowstone Park Foundation, "President Ford Was a Yellowstone Ranger."

5. U.S. Forest Service—Salmon-Challis National Forest, "The Mountain Shoshone or Sheepeater Indians," http://www.fs.usda.gov/detail/scnf/about-forest/districts/?cid=fsbdev3_029679

Chapter 3. A Geology Wonderland

1. U.S. National Park Service—Yellowstone, "Volcano."

2. Jeremy Schmidt and Steven Fuller, *Yellowstone and Grand Teton National Parks Road Guide* (Washington, DC: National Geographic, 2010), p. 14.

3. U.S. National Park Service—Yellowstone, "Geology," http://www.nps.gov/yell/naturescience/geology.htm

Chapter 4. A Living Wildlife Laboratory

1. U.S. National Park Service—Yellowstone, "Wolves in Yellowstone," http://www.nps.gov/yell/naturescience/wolves.htm

2. Don Pitcher, *Moon Handbooks: Yellowstone & Grand Teton* (Emeryville, CA: Avalon Travel Publishing, 2006), p. 316.

3. U.S. National Park Service—Yellowstone, "History of Wildland Fire in Yellowstone."

4. Pitcher, p. 317.

5. Ibid., pp. 316–317.

6. U.S. National Park Service—Yellowstone, "Bear Safety," http://www.nps.gov/yell/planyourvisit/bearsafety.htm

Chapter 5. Adventure All Year Long

1. U.S. National Park Service, "Visitor Use Statistics," https://irma.nps.gov/Stats/Reports/Park

2. U.S. National Park Service—Yellowstone, "Weather," http://www.nps.gov/yell/planyourvisit/weather.htm

3. Mary Forgione, "Did Camera-equipped Drone Crash into Yellowstone's Largest Hot Spring?" *Los Angeles Times,* August 8, 2014, http://www.latimes.com/travel/california/la-trb-yellowstone-drone-hot-spring-20140807-story.html

Works Consulted

Fishbein, Seymour L. *Yellowstone Country: The Enduring Wonder.* Washington, DC: National Geographic Society, 1997.

Fodor's Yellowstone and Grand Teton National Parks. Eds. Debbie Harmsen, Michael Nalepa. New York: Random House, 2010.

Forgione, Mary. "Did Camera-Equipped Drone Crash Into Yellowstone's Largest Hot Springs?" *Los Angeles Times,* August 8, 2014, http://www.latimes.com/travel/california/la-trb-yellowstone-drone-hot-spring-20140807-story.html

Haines, Aubrey L. *Yellowstone National Park: Its Exploration and Establishment.* Washington, D.C.: U.S. Department of the Interior, 1974.

Loendorf, Lawrence L., and Nancy Medaris Stone. *Mountain Spirit: The Sheep Eater Indians of Yellowstone.* Salt Lake City: The University of Utah Press, 2006.

Mayhew, Bradley, Andrew Dean Nystrom, and Amy Marr. *Yellowstone and Grand Teton National Parks.* Victoria, Australia: Lonely Planet, 2003.

Pitcher, Don. *Moon Handbooks: Yellowstone & Grand Teton.* Emeryville, CA: Avalon Travel Publishing, 2006.

Schmidt, Jeremy, and Steven Fuller. *Yellowstone and Grand Teton National Parks Road Guide.* Washington, D.C.: National Geographic, 2010.

U.S. National Park Service. "Grand Teton." U.S. Department of the Interior, http://www.nps.gov/grte/index.htm

—. "NPS Visitor Use Statistics." U.S. Department of the Interior. https://irma.nps.gov/Stats/

—. "Yellowstone." U.S. Department of the Interior, http://www.nps.gov/yell/index.htm

Yellowstone Park Foundation. http://www.ypf.org.

Books

Aretha, David. *Yellowstone National Park: Adventure, Explore, Discover.* Berkeley Heights, NJ: MyReportLinks.com Books, 2009.

Frisch, Nate. *Yellowstone National Park.* North Mankato, MN: Creative Education, 2014.

George, Jean Craighead. *The Wolves Are Back.* New York: Dutton Children's Books, 2008.

Judge, Lita. *Yellowstone Moran: Painting the American West.* New York: Viking, 2009.

McCarthy, Pat. *Friends of the Earth: A History of American Environmentalism with 21 Activities.* Chicago: Chicago Review Press, 2013.

Temple, Teri. *Welcome to Yellowstone National Park.* Chanhassen, MN: Child's World, 2007.

On the Web

National Park Service: Kids in Parks
http://www.nps.gov/kids/index.cfm

Old Faithful Virtual Visitor Center
http://www.nps.gov/features/yell/ofvec/index2.htm

USGS Yellowstone Volcano Observatory Webcams
http://volcanoes.usgs.gov/volcanoes/yellowstone/yellowstone_multimedia_10.html

Yellowstone National Park
http://www.nps.gov/yell/forkids/

Yellowstone Wolf Project
http://www.yellowstone.org/wolf-project/

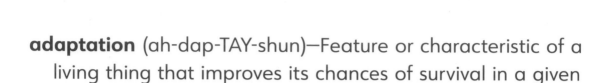

adaptation (ah-dap-TAY-shun)—Feature or characteristic of a living thing that improves its chances of survival in a given environment.

backcountry (BAK-kun-tree)—Wilderness with limited access to modern services (such as electricity, running water, and gas stations).

caldera (kall-DAYR-uh)—Large, sunken area formed at the site of an exploded or collapsed volcano.

continental divide (KON-tin-en-tal dee-VIDE)—An imaginary line that sits atop a ridge of mountains that divide a continent into two main areas.

fumarole (FYOO-muh-rohl)—Volcanic hole in the surface of the Earth that spews steam.

geyser (GY-zer)—Hot spring that occasionally erupts a fountain of water.

glacier (GLAY-shur)—Enormous, slow-moving mass of ice, formed from snow packed down over many winters.

keystone species (KEY-stohn SPEE-sheez)—A species whose presence (or absence) affects many other species in the same ecosystem.

petrified (PEH-trih-fyd)—Changed from once-living material to stone over time.

poacher (POH-chur)—Someone who hunts without proper permission.

prismatic (priz-MAA-tik)—Colored with many bright hues.

temperate (TEM-prit)—Moderate in temperature, neither the hottest nor the coldest.

thermophile (THUR-muh-fyl)—A life form that thrives in an extremely hot environment.

vandalism (VAN-dul-izm)—Damaging or destroying protected property on purpose.